M000196615

Arise, shine, for your light has come,
>   and the glory of the Lord rises upon you.
See, darkness covers the earth
>   and thick darkness is over the peoples,
>   but the Lord rises upon you
>   and his glory appears over you.
Nations will come to your light,
>   and kings to the brightness of your dawn.

>   Isaiah 60:1-3

Tidings of Great Joy:

Devotions for Advent and Christmas

Sharon Pullen

SOPHIA'S HOUSE PUBLICATIONS

Tidings of Great Joy: Devotions for Advent and Christmas

ISBN 978-0-9831179-0-2

Copyright © 2010 by Sharon Pullen

Published by Sophia's House Publications, 2000 Old Crawford Road, Wake Forest, NC 27587

All rights reserved. No part of this book may be reproduced, stored in a retrieval system, distributed, or transmitted in any form or by any means—electronic, mechanical, photocopy, recording, or other—except for brief quotations in printed reviews, without the prior written permission of the publisher.

Unless otherwise noted, all scripture quotations are taken from *The Holy Bible*, New International Version (NIV), copyright © 1973, 1978, 1984, International Bible Society. Used by permission of Zondervan Bible Publishers, all rights reserved.

Other sources include: the New Revised Standard Version of the Bible (NRSV), copyright © 1989, Division of Christian Education of the National Council of Churches of Christ in the United States of America. Used by permission. All rights reserved; The King James Version of the Bible (KJV).

Grateful acknowledgment is given to Mr. Charles Schultz, creator of Peanuts, for the quotation from *A Charlie Brown Christmas*, 1965. Peanuts: © United Feature Syndicate, Inc. Used by permission. All rights reserved.

Cover and interior design by Southern Cross Writing & Editing, Raleigh, NC
Back cover photo by Jordan Pullen

The author may be contacted at smpullen@gmail.com.

Acknowledgments

Many people have helped me produce this book. I wish to thank just a few of the ones who were especially generous with their time and support of the project.

I am very grateful to Paul Koning for his editorial expertise and insights, and for his work on the design and layout of the book. Thanks also to Lisa Gibson, Lisa Arney, and Carolyn Koning, not only for their creative input and assistance on the project, but also for their encouragement and excitement about the book.

I want to express my sincere appreciation to the people of Church of the Holy Cross in Raleigh, North Carolina, for reading the first draft of this book and offering their suggestions, comments, and advice. My special thanks to Janet Robertson, who was instrumental in transferring my ideas for this book from my imagination to the printed page. If she had not had the courage to ask me in August to produce a family devotional *for the upcoming Advent*, many years might have passed before I ever got around to doing it.

Finally, thank you to my husband and children for their willingness to serve as the main test group in using the lessons for family devotions and for their honesty and encouragement. I hope I will never take for granted the blessing of having a family who loves me and understands my need to write.

Table of Contents

Foreword

A few years ago, just before Christmas, I was shopping at a local mall. I was surrounded by all the sights and sounds of our secular holiday season—tense shoppers in a rush, glitzy decorations everywhere, stores enticing customers to spend more money than they have on things they don't need. And down the mall, I could see a long line of tired parents standing with their children who were waiting to tell Santa Claus all their material wishes. I found myself wondering what God thought about this whole holiday scene. How did He feel about the way our culture celebrates the birth of His Son? None of it seemed to have much to do with Jesus. So I prayed, "Lord, what do you think of all this? And what do you think of me for participating in it?" I was almost afraid to hear His answer. You see, in spite of all the commercialization of Christmas, I love the holidays. I love the festive mood, the parties, the presents, and the sparkling lights and decorations. But I also love the quiet, reverent holiness of the season; and I was feeling uneasy, wondering if I was allowing all the festivities to distract me from the holiness.

I sensed the Lord saying, *"Listen."*

"Listen to what?" I asked.

"Listen."

So I stepped out of the flow of people and stopped just inside the entrance to a store. I could still hear all the noises of the mall, but underneath it all I could also hear—*music.*

Over the speaker system, I could hear these words being sung:

> Glory streams from Heaven afar.
> Heavenly hosts sing Alleluia.
> Christ the Savior is born.
> Christ the Savior is born.

Silent night,
Holy night.
Son of God, love's pure light.
Radiant beams from thy holy face
With the dawn of redeeming grace.
Jesus, Lord at thy birth.
Jesus, Lord at thy birth.

The Lord said, *"At what other time of year do you hear my name proclaimed so clearly?"*

And He was right. Just a few minutes earlier, I had passed a children's choir performing "Joy to the World" in the center of the mall. And soon I would watch one of my favorite Christmas shows with my children. Right there on network TV each year at about this time, Charlie Brown cries out in frustration, "Isn't there anyone who knows what Christmas is all about?" And Linus answers, "Sure, Charlie Brown, I can tell you what Christmas is all about." Then he recites from Luke 2:

> And there were in the same country shepherds abiding in the field, keeping watch over their flock by night. And, lo, the angel of the Lord came upon them, and the glory of the Lord shone round about them: and they were sore afraid. And the angel said unto them, Fear not: for behold, I bring you tidings of great joy, which shall be to all people. For unto you is born this day in the city of David a Saviour, which is Christ the Lord. And this shall be a sign unto you; Ye shall find the babe wrapped in swaddling clothes, lying in a manger. And suddenly there was with the angel a multitude of the heavenly host praising God, and saying, Glory to God in the highest, and on earth peace, good will toward men.

"That's what Christmas is all about, Charlie Brown."

That IS what Christmas is all about. As usual, a lot of noise and glitz will threaten to distract us during the holidays. The season is far from silent, and yet the words of "Silent Night" can still be heard. The enemy of God is trying his utmost to drown out the real message of Christmas, but it's still there. You just have to step out of the flow for a moment, stop, and listen.

That's why I wrote this book. So that we can be still and quiet for a few minutes every day and listen to the real meaning of Advent and Christmas. We all have to decide for ourselves how much we will participate in the secular celebration of the holidays, but I believe we can enjoy the things we love about our cultural traditions and still remain focused on the coming of Jesus.

I began writing this book as a way to help families with children draw together for a time of daily family devotions during the holidays, but I quickly realized that the profound message of God's expression of love for His people really cannot be oversimplified. All of us—married, single, young, old, with or without children—need a time to stop and listen to the incredible story of God's gift to us in the coming of Jesus. With this in mind, I have tried to make the daily format of these devotions flexible and adaptable to everyone who uses them.

The Advent devotions are organized around four themes, one for each of the four weeks in Advent. Then, beginning on Christmas Day, you will find a daily devotion for each of the 12 days of Christmas. The book is designed to be used with an Advent wreath, and I think your devotion time would be enhanced by practicing this ancient tradition, but certainly you can still benefit from the daily discipline of prayer and scripture reading without using a wreath.

Each daily entry includes an opening prayer, a scripture reference for you to look up and read, a short lesson, key verses from the reading, and a closing prayer. You are, of course, free to use your own prayers or add to mine. If you are using this book with a baby or a very young child, you might skip the lessons and focus on reading the scriptures, or even just the key verses, to the child. Parents of older children might want to encourage the kids to memorize some of the key verses or to participate by reading aloud. Use this book to suit your needs. Even if you use only the scripture references to guide you in your daily Bible reading, you will be able to hear the amazing story of the coming of Jesus into the world to save His people.

Advent begins four Sundays before Christmas. If you plan to use a wreath, you will want to have it decorated by then and set up wherever you plan to do your devotions. For a more complete explanation of this tradition, please read the section titled "The Advent Wreath." If you are using this book with your children, read the next two sections aloud to them before beginning the devotions on the first day of Advent.

I pray that God will use this book to bless you in your private or group devotions with a new understanding and appreciation of the richness of this season called Advent, so that when Christmas arrives, your joy will be complete.

May Christ dwell in your hearts this holiday season.

Sharon

Happy New Year!

But wait. Isn't the New Year still a month away? According to the calendar on your wall, yes. But this is the beginning of the new church year. Advent is the first season we celebrate in the life of the church, and it begins four Sundays before Christmas. The word *Advent* comes from the Latin word *Adventus*, which means "coming." Jesus is coming.

You are probably beginning to think about Christmas and all the things you like to do—sing carols, decorate your tree, wrap gifts, bake cookies. Everyone seems very busy preparing for Christmas. But the season of Advent is really meant to be a time of quiet preparation when we reflect on the greatness of the gift God gave us when he sent His Son, Jesus, into the world. Advent is also a time when we prepare for Jesus' second coming. He promised that He would come again, this time not as a child, but as a King.

It's hard to be quiet and still and think about Jesus with all the excitement of preparing for Christmas. And that's what this book is all about. We are going to set aside just a little time each day during Advent to read the Bible and think about the amazing gift God gave us when He sent Jesus into the world and about the wonderful promise that Jesus will come again. And we won't stop after Christmas Day, because that is only the beginning of Christmas. We will continue to read what the Bible says about the birth of Jesus and about His coming again all the way past New Year's Day on your calendar. We can enjoy all the excitement and activities of the holidays while still giving Jesus His rightful place as King in our lives and making Him the focus of our Christmas celebration.

The Advent Wreath

If you are using an Advent wreath during your devotion time, you should know that the history of this decoration dates back much further than your Christmas tree or any of the other decorations you have in your home during the holidays. Many different traditions and stories about Advent wreaths have been passed down, and you might have heard various explanations about the symbolism of the wreath. The readings in this book were selected and organized so that you can use a wreath to enhance your devotion times, but you certainly can use this book without using a wreath or candles. Or you can light a different type of candle, whatever best creates the mood for this time you have set aside for the Lord. The Bible does not mention Advent wreaths, and the traditions surrounding them have changed over time, but most of these traditions are grounded in scripture and come from a desire on the part of God's people to focus on the coming of Jesus during the season of Advent.

The circular shape of the wreath represents God's unending love for us, and the evergreens traditionally used to decorate the wreath symbolize the eternal life that God offers us through His Son, Jesus. Notice the colors of the candles. Purple represents the royalty of Jesus our King. Purple is also the color of penitence and reminds us to examine ourselves, confess our sins, receive the forgiveness God gives through Jesus, and prepare ourselves for His coming again. Rose (pink) represents the joy we have in Jesus. And white represents the purity of Jesus, who was without sin. On each of the four Sundays in Advent, we will light a new candle. Each candle represents a different theme, and the Bible readings during Advent will focus on the four themes represented by the three purple candles and the one pink candle: Hope, Peace, Joy, and Love. The white candle is called the Christ candle, and we won't light it until Christmas Eve when we celebrate the birth of Jesus. Each time we light a new candle, we will continue to light the old ones, so that by the time Christmas comes, the whole wreath will be lit. The growing brightness of our wreath is meant to symbolize our growing anticipation of the coming of Jesus. The time of celebrating his birth is getting closer, and the time of His coming again is also getting closer. Jesus is called the light of the world, so with each passing week, the light is growing brighter.

Lessons

Hope

Read Isaiah 9:2–7 aloud, and light the first purple candle.

Opening Prayer Almighty God, you sent your Son to be the light of the world, to give us hope, and to show us the way back to you in a dark world. Open our eyes to the truth of your Word as we read the promises you made to our forefathers in the faith to send a Savior into the world. Fill us with hope in Jesus. *Amen.*

Lesson The first candle in the Advent wreath is called the Hope candle. This week our Bible readings will remind us of the hope we have in God's promise to send a Savior to His people. We will read about the people who lived long before Jesus was born—the patriarchs of the Old Testament who waited and hoped for the Savior to arrive.

Read Romans 15:4–13.

Today, over 2,000 years after Jesus was born just as God promised, our hope is still in Jesus. He is still the light of the world who shows us the way to the Father and gives us hope as we wait for His second coming.

The world is beginning to celebrate the holiday season. Look around this week at all the decorations that are going up in the stores, on houses, in yards, on street corners, and in your school or your workplace. Notice all the lights? This year, try to keep your mind on Jesus. Every time you see the lights of holiday decorations in your own home and out in the world, think of Jesus—the light of the world—and remember the hope we have in Him.

Closing Prayer May the God of hope fill us with all joy and peace as we trust in Him, so that we may overflow with hope by the power of the Holy Spirit. *Amen.*

In the Beginning

Light the first purple candle.

Opening Prayer   Almighty God, you sent your Son to be the light of the world, to give us hope, and to show us the way back to you in a dark world. Open our eyes to the truth of your Word as we read the promises you made to our forefathers in the faith to send a Savior into the world. Fill us with hope in Jesus. *Amen.*

Lesson   The best place to begin is at the beginning.

Read John 1:1–14.

Before our world was made, Jesus was there. He was with God, and He was God. All things were made through Him, John tells us. The earth, sun and stars, plants, animals, and people—nothing existed before He did. The man who wrote these words was one of Jesus' disciples. While Jesus was living here with us as a man, John was one of His best friends. (The man John refers to in verse 6 is called John the Baptist—a relative of Jesus who we will learn about later.) Not only did God give John the disciple a close friendship with Jesus, but He also gave him a wonderful understanding of who Jesus really is so that he could explain it to both the Jews and the Gentiles. The word *gentile* means one who is far away—a foreigner. In the Bible, a Gentile is anyone who is not Jewish. To the Jewish people who were waiting for the Savior to come, John was saying that Jesus took part in God's creation of the world, that

He is the one who spoke through the prophets and about whom the prophets spoke. He is the Word of God, and that Word became flesh and lived among us for a time. Most of the Gentiles John was writing to either believed there were many different gods or no gods at all, but they did believe that some kind of governing force, some central source of life, gave meaning to the universe. The word they used to describe this force was *Logos*, which is Greek for *the Word*. John was saying to these Gentiles that Jesus is this governing force for which they were looking. He is the source of all life, and there are no other gods before Him. John said that all people, Jews and Gentiles, who believe in Jesus, will become children of God.

Key Verses
In the beginning was the Word, and the Word was with God, and the Word was God. He was with God in the beginning. Through him all things were made; without him nothing was made that has been made. *John 1:1–3*

Closing Prayer
Lord Jesus, thank you for coming into the world full of grace and truth, and for granting us the right to become children of God. *Amen.*

Our Beginning

Light the first purple candle.

Opening Prayer Almighty God, you sent your Son to be the light of the world, to give us hope, and to show us the way back to you in a dark world. Open our eyes to the truth of your Word as we read the promises you made to our forefathers in the faith to send a Savior into the world. Fill us with hope in Jesus. *Amen.*

Lesson Yesterday we read that Jesus has existed from the very beginning. He became one of us when He was born into the world as a baby, but that was not His beginning. We also read that all things were made through Him and that nothing was made without Him. That means He must have been there when *we* were made.

Read Genesis 1: 26–31.

In verse 26, God said, "Let us make man in our image...." Who is *us?*

God the Father, God the Son, and God the Holy Spirit were all present at the creation. When John said that through Jesus all things were made, that includes us. Jesus was with God long before we were created, and He was present on the sixth day of creation when we were made. When God looked at all he had made, He saw that it was very good. We are created in His image, and from the very first moment of our existence, He loved us, accepted us, and was willing to do anything to keep us with Him.

Key Verses　So God created man in his own image, in the image of God he created him; male and female he created them. *Genesis 1:27*

Closing Prayer　Lord Jesus, you have known us from our very beginning. As we draw near to you in this holy season, reveal yourself to us. *Amen.*

Abraham's Blessing

Light the first purple candle.

Opening Almighty God, you sent your Son to be the light of
Prayer the world, to give us hope, and to show us the way
back to you in a dark world. Open our eyes to the
truth of your Word as we read the promises you
made to our forefathers in the faith to send a Savior
into the world. Fill us with hope in Jesus. *Amen.*

Lesson God created us to enjoy a perfect relationship with
Him, but He gave us the freedom to choose
whether or not to obey Him. Man was deceived by
Satan, who had turned away from God and made
himself God's enemy. When we chose to disobey
God, our perfect relationship with Him was ruined.
What follows the Fall of Man is a sad story of our
separation from the One who created us and the
misery that resulted from that separation. But even
then, God still loved us and was not willing to let us
live apart from him forever.

He had a plan to bring us back.

Read Genesis 12:1–5 and 15:1–6.

God's plan from the beginning has been to make
Himself known to all people. God chose Abram,
whom He later renamed Abraham, to become the
father of the Israelites. Even though Abraham and
his wife, Sarah, seemed too old to have children,
God gave them a son and kept His promise to bless

the whole world through Abraham. Many generations later, Jesus was born as a descendant of
Abraham to show us the way back to God.

Key   The Lord had said to Abram, "I will make you into
Verses   a great nation and I will bless you; I will make your
name great, and you will be a blessing. I will bless
those who bless you, and whoever curses you I will
curse; and all peoples on earth will be blessed
through you." *Genesis 12:1a, 2–3*

Closing   Lord God, you kept your promise to bless all people
Prayer   through Abraham. Help us to believe you and to put
our hope in your promises to us. *Amen.*

The Great 1 AM

Light the first purple candle.

Opening Prayer Almighty God, you sent your Son to be the light of the world, to give us hope, and to show us the way back to you in a dark world. Open our eyes to the truth of your Word as we read the promises you made to our forefathers in the faith to send a Savior into the world. Fill us with hope in Jesus. *Amen.*

Lesson Hundreds of years had passed since God made His promise to Abraham, and the people of God had become slaves in Egypt, but God had not forgotten His people or His promise.

Read Exodus 3:1–15.

God called Moses to lead the Israelites from slavery in Egypt to a land where they could be free. When Moses asked God what he should say to the people if they were to ask who would deliver them, God answered, "I AM WHO I AM. This is what you are to say to the Israelites: 'I AM has sent me to you.'" The ancient Hebrew word God used to name Himself is hard to understand in English. Perhaps the best transliteration for this particular name of God is "I WAS THEN, I AM NOW, I WILL BE FOREVER." God was telling Moses that He had not changed and that he never will. He is the One who made us and who called Abraham, and He does not change or forget His promises. He was continuing to keep His promises through Moses, and He is continuing to keep His promises to us today.

Key Verses   God said to Moses, "I AM WHO I AM. This is my name forever, the name by which I am to be remembered from generation to generation."
Exodus 3:14a, 15b

Closing Prayer   God, you are the great "I AM," the One who was, and is, and will be forever. *Amen.*

The House of David

Light the first purple candle.

Opening Prayer Almighty God, you sent your Son to be the light of the world, to give us hope, and to show us the way back to you in a dark world. Open our eyes to the truth of your Word as we read the promises you made to our forefathers in the faith to send a Savior into the world. Fill us with hope in Jesus. *Amen.*

Lesson Hundreds of years had passed since Moses led the Israelites out of Egypt, and God was still working out His plan to save His people.

Read 2 Samuel 7:4–29.

God chose David to become the king of Israel, and He promised David that through his offspring, He would establish a kingdom that would last forever. David was a man like all the other patriarchs—he made mistakes and did not always obey God. But God chose him and worked through him to accomplish His will in the same way He works through us even though we make mistakes. David's prayer gives us a glimpse into the reason God chose him. God said to David, "Now I will make your name great, like the names of the greatest men of the earth." But David replies, "Do as you promised, so that *your* name will be great forever" (emphasis mine). God did keep His promise to make an everlasting kingdom from the house of David. Jesus, a direct descendant of David, was born about 1,000 years later, and His kingdom will have no end.

Key Verses   Then King David went in and sat before the Lord, and he said: "And now, Lord God, keep forever the promise you have made concerning your servant and his house. Do as you promised, so that your name will be great forever. Then men will say, 'The Lord Almighty is God over Israel!' And the house of your servant David will be established before you." *2 Samuel 7:18a, 25–26*

Closing Prayer   Lord God, your name will be great forever. *Amen.*

Review

Light the first purple candle.

Opening Prayer   Almighty God, you sent your Son to be the light of the world, to give us hope, and to show us the way back to you in a dark world. Open our eyes to the truth of your Word as we read the promises you made to our forefathers in the faith to send a Savior into the world. Fill us with hope in Jesus. *Amen.*

Lesson   Our theme this week was Hope, and our lessons focused on the promises God made to care for His people and never to leave them. The Israelites hoped and waited for God to fulfill His promise to send a Savior into the world, and we know that He kept this promise when Jesus was born. We learned that Jesus has been with the Father from the beginning. He came the first time just as God promised, and He will come again. Like the patriarchs of the Old Testament, our hope is in the faithfulness of God to keep His promises.

Each Saturday, before beginning a new week in Advent, we will review the key verses for the concluding week. Read each passage aloud, and hear the hope in the promises of God.

Key Verses   In the beginning was the Word, and the Word was with God, and the Word was God. He was with God in the beginning. Through him all things were made; without him nothing was made that has been made. *John 1:1–3*

So God created man in his own image, in the image of God he created him; male and female he created them. *Genesis 1:27*

The Lord had said to Abram, "I will make you into a great nation and I will bless you; I will make your name great, and you will be a blessing. I will bless those who bless you, and whoever curses you I will curse; and all peoples on earth will be blessed through you." *Genesis 12:1a, 2–3*

God said to Moses, "I AM WHO I AM. This is my name forever, the name by which I am to be remembered from generation to generation." *Exodus 3:14a, 15b*

Then King David went in and sat before the Lord, and he said: "And now, Lord God, keep forever the promise you have made concerning your servant and his house. Do as you promised, so that your name will be great forever. Then men will say, 'The Lord Almighty is God over Israel!' And the house of your servant David will be established before you." *2 Samuel 7:18a, 25–26*

Closing Prayer May the God of hope fill us with all joy and peace as we trust in Him, so that we may overflow with hope by the power of the Holy Spirit. *Amen.*

Peace

Read Isaiah 9:2–7 aloud, and light the first and second purple candles.

Opening Prayer Lord Jesus, you are the Prince of Peace, and your reign of righteousness will be forever and ever. Help us today to hear your Word and to understand the promises you made through the prophets of old. As we await your coming again, fill us with hope in you, and grant us your peace. *Amen.*

Lesson The second purple candle in the Advent wreath is called the Peace candle. This week our Bible readings will remind us of the peace that Jesus brings when He comes. We will read some of the prophecies from the Old Testament which foretold the coming of the Savior centuries before Jesus was born.

Read Jeremiah 33:14–16.

When God speaks, things happen just as He says. God's Word is true even if we do not completely understand it or if things happen in a way we do not expect. God spoke through the prophets about the coming of Jesus. He said through Jeremiah that the days were coming when He would fulfill the promises He had made to His people. Sometimes when God spoke to His people about things that had not yet happened, He was referring to more than one event in history. Remember that God has no beginning and no end, and Jesus has always been with the Father. God sees history—from the creation until the time Jesus comes again—all at the same time. When God spoke through the prophets of the Old Testament about the coming of Jesus, he was not only talking about the time when Jesus would be born into the world as a baby. He also was talking about the time when Jesus will come again as a King to gather all His people and bring peace to the world. As we read how these prophets foretold the coming of Jesus, you will begin to see the twofold nature of these prophecies.

Closing Prayer Lord God, you have spoken through the prophets about the coming of Jesus, and all your words are true. *Amen.*

Jesus Brings Peace

Light the first two purple candles.

Opening Prayer Lord Jesus, you are the Prince of Peace, and your reign of righteousness will be forever and ever. Help us today to hear your Word and to understand the promises you made through the prophets of old. As we await your coming again, fill us with hope in you, and grant us your peace. *Amen.*

Lesson Isaiah was a great prophet who foretold the coming of the Messiah over 700 years before Jesus was born.

Read Isaiah 2:1–5.

You can see why the Jewish people living during the time of Jesus' earthly ministry might have been confused about who He was. They had heard the things Isaiah and the other prophets had written about the coming Messiah, and they were expecting a king who would lead his people into a time of great peace. When Jesus did not bring peace to the earth in the way they had envisioned, some of the Jews concluded that He was not the promised Savior He claimed to be. Isaiah had foretold the coming of the Savior into the world, and he had described the events that would take place when Jesus was born. Furthermore, and more difficult for the Jews to comprehend, Isaiah also had described a time when Jesus would come again. Jesus was born according to Isaiah's prophecies about His birth, but

He accomplished His earthly ministry, died, rose again, and went to be with the Father without bringing the kind of world peace described by Isaiah. The time when the world will live in peace with Jesus as our King will not happen until after He comes again.

But Jesus did bring peace when He came the first time—a peace different from the kind some people expected. He promised that anyone who believed in Him would have the assurance of eternal life and peace in their hearts even in times of trouble. When He comes again, He will bring peace to the whole earth, but He gives peace *now* to those who follow Him—not the world's idea of peace, but something far better. Jesus said, "Peace I leave with you; my peace I give you. I do not give to you as the world gives. Do not let your hearts be troubled and do not be afraid." (*John 14:27*)

Key Verses "Come, let us go up to the mountain of the Lord, to the house of the God of Jacob. He will teach us his ways, so that we may walk in his paths." *Isaiah 2:3*

Closing Prayer Lord Jesus, thank you for giving us your peace. *Amen.*

The Branch of Jesse

Light the first two purple candles.

Opening Prayer
Lord Jesus, you are the Prince of Peace, and your reign of righteousness will be forever and ever. Help us today to hear your Word and to understand the promises you made through the prophets of old. As we await your coming again, fill us with hope in you, and grant us your peace. *Amen.*

Lesson
The prophet Isaiah foretold the coming of Jesus—both His first and His second comings.

Read Isaiah 11:1–10.

God promised David that He would establish his house forever. Approximately 400 years after God made this promise, the Israelites were taken captive by the Babylonians, the last king who was descended from David died, and the earthly kingdom that God had established through David ended. It seemed God was not going to fulfill the promise He had made to David. But God kept the Israelites together, and we can trace the descendants of David even through the time of the Babylonian captivity. Isaiah said that a shoot would grow up from the stump of Jesse, who was David's father, and that the branch that grew would become a King who would reign forever. David's dynasty was like a tree that had been cut down and appeared to be dead, but God still kept His promise. Jesus was born into the family of Joseph and Mary, who were both direct descendants of David.

Key Verses   A shoot will come up from the stump of Jesse; from his roots a Branch will bear fruit. *Isaiah 11:1*

Closing Prayer   Lord Jesus, you are the Root and the Offspring of David, and your Kingdom will have no end. *Amen.*

A Virgin Will Give Birth

Note to Parents: Please preview this lesson to prepare for possible questions.

Light the first two purple candles.

Opening Prayer Lord Jesus, you are the Prince of Peace, and your reign of righteousness will be forever and ever. Help us today to hear your Word and to understand the promises you made through the prophets of old. As we await your coming again, fill us with hope in you, and grant us your peace. *Amen.*

Lesson God promised a sign to help us recognize the Savior.

Read Isaiah 7:10–14.

Remember that the Old Testament prophecies often had more than one meaning and sometimes predicted a soon-to-occur event as well as a more distant future event. The people who first heard this prophecy probably interpreted it in light of current events happening under the rule of King Ahaz. But when they heard the part about a virgin giving birth, they must have shaken their heads in disbelief. It would be impossible for a young woman who had never been intimate with a man to have a child. Yet we know that many centuries later, God chose Mary, a virgin, to give birth to His Son Jesus, who is called Immanuel—God with us. Hundreds of years later, the Gospel writer Matthew quoted Isaiah 7:14

to show that the long-term prediction of Isaiah's prophecy was fulfilled when Mary gave birth to Jesus (*Matthew 1:23*).

Key Verses Therefore the Lord himself will give you a sign: The virgin will be with child and will give birth to a son, and will call him Immanuel. *Isaiah 7:14*

Closing Prayer Immanuel, God with us, you are the fulfillment of all God's promises. *Amen.*

Bethlehem

Light the first two purple candles.

Opening Prayer Lord Jesus, you are the Prince of Peace, and your reign of righteousness will be forever and ever. Help us today to hear your Word and to understand the promises you made through the prophets of old. As we await your coming again, fill us with hope in you, and grant us your peace. *Amen.*

Lesson *Read Micah 5:2–5a.*

Bethlehem is a small town about 5 miles south of Jerusalem (Ephrathah was the name of the district). Jesus was born in a region with a long history of conflict. For many centuries, wars and battles had raged in and around Jerusalem. Even today in that part of the world, the fighting continues. When Jesus was born, this region was ruled by the Roman Empire. The Romans had conquered vast territories and were now satisfied that they ruled the entire civilized world. The fighting had stopped, and the Romans were busy running their huge empire. Unlike some of the conquerors of that time, the Romans allowed the people they conquered to keep their customs and practices, as long as they paid taxes to the government and obeyed all Roman laws. Therefore, the Jewish people were able to practice their faith, have their own leaders, and remain together even though they were governed by the local Roman officials.

Caesar Augustus, the Roman emperor at that time, ordered a census to be taken of all the people living under Roman rule. In order to obey this decree, the Jews returned to the birthplace of their ancestors to be counted. Both Mary and Joseph were descendants of David, so they traveled from their home in Nazareth to Bethlehem, David's birthplace. Because Mary was nearly ready to give birth when she and Joseph made their journey, Jesus was born in Bethlehem, just as the prophets had predicted. This era in history is often called the *Pax Romana*, which means the "Roman Peace." Never before or since has this part of the world experienced such a time of peace. And it was in this place and during this time of unprecedented peace that God sent the Prince of Peace into the world to live among us.

Key Verses   "But you, Bethlehem Ephrathah, though you are small among the clans of Judah, out of you will come for me one who will be ruler over Israel, whose origins are from of old, from ancient times." *Micah 5:2*

Closing Prayer   Lord Jesus, you are the promised One, whose origins are from of old. *Amen.*

Prepare the Way

Light the first two purple candles.

Opening Prayer
Lord Jesus, you are the Prince of Peace, and your reign of righteousness will be forever and ever. Help us today to hear your Word and to understand the promises you made through the prophets of old. As we await your coming again, fill us with hope in you, and grant us your peace. *Amen.*

Lesson
The Old Testament prophets prepared the way for Jesus to come by foretelling his birth and describing his reign of peace. They also proclaimed that God would send a messenger when the time of the Messiah was near.

Read Isaiah 40:1–9.

Next week, we will read about the birth of John the Baptist, who prepared the way for the Messiah as Isaiah predicted by preceding Jesus in birth and by proclaiming to the Jewish people that Jesus was the Christ. We can see that the birth of Jesus happened as the prophets said it would. We know that Jesus was born to a virgin in the town of Bethlehem and that John was the messenger who went before Him. We can look back and see that God sent Jesus into the world just as He said He would.

In the New Testament, the Gospel writer Mark quotes this passage from Isaiah when he tells of the ministry of John the Baptist (*Mark 1:2–3*). God used

John's birth as a sign of the imminent arrival of Jesus, and when the two were grown, it was John who announced the beginning of Jesus' earthly ministry. Isaiah said, "The mouth of the Lord has spoken." And centuries later, Mark echoes the words of the prophet Isaiah and then says, "And so John came." When God speaks, things happen according to His word.

Key Verses A voice of one calling: "In the desert prepare the way for the Lord; make straight in the wilderness a highway for our God. Every valley shall be raised up, every mountain and hill made low; the rough ground shall become level, the rugged places a plain. And the glory of the Lord will be revealed, and all mankind together will see it. For the mouth of the Lord has spoken." *Isaiah 40:3–5*

Closing Prayer Lord, you have spoken. *Amen.*

Review

Light the first two purple candles.

Opening Prayer Lord Jesus, you are the Prince of Peace, and your reign of righteousness will be forever and ever. Help us today to hear your Word and to understand the promises you made through the prophets of old. As we await your coming again, fill us with hope in you, and grant us your peace. *Amen.*

Lesson We can look back and see how God's promises were fulfilled when Jesus was born. We also must look ahead and believe that God will keep His promises about the future. This week we have read the prophecies of the coming of Jesus—both his birth and his second coming. He came the first time just as God said He would, and He will come again just as God says He will. The prophets proclaimed that Jesus would bring peace. When He comes again, He will bring peace to all the earth. But He has brought peace already to the hearts of those who believe in Him and wait expectantly for Him to come again.

Review the key verses for this week. Read them aloud, and let the Lord fill you with peace. He is faithful to keep His promises.

Key Verses "Come, let us go up to the mountain of the Lord, to the house of the God of Jacob. He will teach us his ways, so that we may walk in his paths." *Isaiah 2:3*

A shoot will come up from the stump of Jesse; from his roots a Branch will bear fruit. *Isaiah 11:1*

Therefore the Lord himself will give you a sign: The virgin will be with child and will give birth to a son, and will call him Immanuel. *Isaiah 7:14*

"But you, Bethlehem Ephrathah, though you are small among the clans of Judah, out of you will come for me one who will be ruler over Israel, whose origins are from of old, from ancient times." *Micah 5:2*

A voice of one calling: "In the desert prepare the way for the Lord; make straight in the wilderness a highway for our God. Every valley shall be raised up, every mountain and hill made low; the rough ground shall become level, the rugged places a plain. And the glory of the Lord will be revealed, and all mankind together will see it. For the mouth of the Lord has spoken." *Isaiah 40:3–5*

Closing Prayer   Lord God, you have spoken through the prophets about the coming of Jesus, and all your words are true. *Amen.*

Joy

Read Isaiah 9:2–7 aloud, and light the first two purple candles and the pink candle.

Opening Prayer Lord Jesus, we rejoice in you. As we hear the familiar stories of those who lived in the days of your first coming, open our hearts to experience the joy you brought to your people when you came into the world to live among us. Fill us with hope, grant us your peace, and make us joyful. *Amen.*

Lesson The third Sunday in Advent is called Gaudete Sunday on the traditional church calendar. The word *gaudete* is Latin and means "rejoice." The pink candle in our Advent wreath is called the Joy candle. Today we will read from both the Old and New Testaments to mark the transition we will make this week. Until now, we have read about the people who waited and watched for the Savior long before He arrived. This week, we will read about those people who were eyewitnesses to the birth of Jesus and who experienced the joy of seeing God fulfill His promise.

Read Zephaniah 3:14–20 and Philippians 4:4–7.

Christmas is coming! We feel joy in our anticipation of celebrating the birth of Jesus, and because Jesus has come and is coming again, we can have joy in Him forever.

Closing Prayer   Lord Jesus, our joy is complete in you. *Amen.*

Zechariah and Elizabeth

Light the first two purple candles and the pink candle.

Opening Prayer
Lord Jesus, we rejoice in you. As we hear the familiar stories of those who lived in the days of your first coming, open our hearts to experience the joy you brought to your people when you came into the world to live among us. Fill us with hope, grant us your peace, and make us joyful. *Amen.*

Lesson
We ended last week by reading the prophecy that God would send a messenger to prepare the way for Jesus, and we will begin this week by reading about the fulfillment of that prophecy. God chose Zechariah to be the father of the promised messenger who would come before Jesus and who later would announce that Jesus was the Christ. Zechariah and his wife, Elizabeth, were old and childless. People believed during those times that God had withheld His blessing from a couple if He had not given them children. But this must have been a mystery to those who knew Zechariah and Elizabeth, because they were known to be holy and upright people. Zechariah was a priest who served in the temple, and he was required to go to Jerusalem twice a year to perform his duties. On the trip we will read about today in Luke's Gospel, Zechariah was chosen for a once-in-a-lifetime opportunity that brought him and his family great honor. When the priests cast lots for the privilege of going into the most holy place in the temple to burn

incense to the Lord, Zechariah was the one chosen.

Read Luke 1:5–25.

For what do you think Zechariah had been praying? For a child? For the Messiah to come? We do not know exactly what he had been praying for, but we know God did both of these things. Even though Elizabeth was past the age of bearing children, God gave her a son. He told Zechariah that this child would bring great joy, not only to his parents, but also to all the people he would lead to Jesus.

Key Verses   But the angel said to him: "Do not be afraid, Zechariah; your prayer has been heard. Your wife Elizabeth will bear you a son, and you are to give him the name John. He will be a joy and delight to you, and many will rejoice because of his birth." *Luke 1:13–14*

Closing Prayer   Lord God, your blessings bring us joy. *Amen.*

Mary and the Angel Gabriel

Note to Parents: Please preview this lesson to prepare for possible questions.

Light the first two purple candles and the pink candle.

Opening Prayer — Lord Jesus, we rejoice in you. As we hear the familiar stories of those who lived in the days of your first coming, open our hearts to experience the joy you brought to your people when you came into the world to live among us. Fill us with hope, grant us your peace, and make us joyful. *Amen.*

Lesson — Mary was a young woman who was betrothed (engaged) to a man named Joseph. But she was still too young to be married—probably about 14—and she was still living at home with her parents. Her story is amazing and unique. Several times in the Bible, couples who seemed too old to have children (Abraham and Sarah, Zechariah and Elizabeth) were blessed by God with a baby. Those were certainly miracles from God, but what happened to Mary had never happened to anyone. Never before or since has a virgin given birth. This is one way we can be positive that Jesus was the Son of God.

Read Luke 1:26–38.

Mary's answer to Gabriel's pronouncement tells us all we need to know about why God chose her to be the mother of Jesus. The angel told her she was going to have a baby, and she simply wanted to know how this was going to be accomplished. She knew it could not happen in the usual way, because she was not married. When the angel described to her how it would happen, rather than being terrified as most young girls might have been, Mary answered that God could do whatever He wanted with her.

Key Verses   The angel answered, "The Holy Spirit will come upon you, and the power of the Most High will overshadow you. So the holy one to be born will be called the Son of God."

"I am the Lord's servant," Mary answered. "May it be to me as you have said." *Luke 1:35, 38*

Closing Prayer   Lord Jesus, you are the Son of God. *Amen.*

Mary Visits Elizabeth

Light the first two purple candles and the pink candle.

Opening Prayer Lord Jesus, we rejoice in you. As we hear the familiar stories of those who lived in the days of your first coming, open our hearts to experience the joy you brought to your people when you came into the world to live among us. Fill us with hope, grant us your peace, and make us joyful. *Amen.*

Lesson Zechariah's wife, Elizabeth, was one of Mary's relatives. Soon after Mary received the news from the angel that she was going to have a child and that Elizabeth also was expecting a baby, she went to visit Elizabeth. We can assume that Elizabeth did not yet know the circumstances of Mary's pregnancy. But God gave Elizabeth the knowledge and understanding that Mary's baby was the long-awaited Messiah.

Read Luke 1:39–56.

Mary must have been greatly encouraged and comforted by Elizabeth's greeting. By this time, she was probably worried that her family and friends would not believe what the angel had told her about the baby she was carrying. For her relative to greet her as "the mother of my Lord" must have reassured her that God's promise to her was true. In response to Elizabeth's greeting, Mary expressed some of the most famous words in the Bible. Her praise to God is sometimes called "The Song of

Mary" or the *Magnificat*, which is Latin for "magnify." They have been written into songs and prayers in the church for centuries, because they are such a beautiful expression of joy.

Key Verses   And Mary said, "My soul magnifies the Lord, and my spirit rejoices in God my Savior, for he has looked with favor on the lowliness of his servant. Surely, from now on all generations will call me blessed; for the Mighty One has done great things for me, and holy is his name." *Luke 1:46–49 (NRSV)*

Closing Prayer   God, you are the Mighty One. Holy is your name. *Amen.*

Joseph

Note to Parents: Please preview this lesson to prepare for possible questions.

Light the first two purple candles and the pink candle.

Opening Prayer Lord Jesus, we rejoice in you. As we hear the familiar stories of those who lived in the days of your first coming, open our hearts to experience the joy you brought to your people when you came into the world to live among us. Fill us with hope, grant us your peace, and make us joyful. *Amen.*

Lesson With all the excitement over the angel's announcement to Mary and Mary's visit with Elizabeth, it is easy to forget about Joseph. He was engaged to Mary and was waiting for her to be old enough to leave her family and become his wife. What do you think he thought when he found out Mary was going to have a baby?

Read Matthew 1:18–25.

Joseph must have experienced painful disappointment over the prospect of breaking his engagement to Mary. In those days, an engagement was very serious and binding—breaking one was not simply a matter of saying you had changed your mind and did not want to get married after all. And it was not at all acceptable for a woman to have a baby before she was married; Mary would have been in a lot of trouble with the Jewish leaders. We can see what a kind man Joseph was in the way he responded to the news that Mary was pregnant. Even though he was hurt and humiliated, he was trying to find a way to end his engagement with Mary without hurting her or creating a scandal. We can also see what a strong and faithful man he was in the way he responded to the angel's message. Although there may have been many who did not believe Mary's story, Joseph believed the words of the angel and did what God told him to do. The last time we hear about Joseph in the Bible is when Jesus was 12, and we do not know how much longer Joseph lived. But we do know that he obeyed God, married Mary, raised and trained Jesus, and served God as a good earthly father.

Key Verses "Joseph son of David, do not be afraid to take Mary home as your wife, because what is conceived in her is from the Holy Spirit. She will give birth to a son, and you are to give him the name Jesus, because he will save his people from their sins." *Matthew 1:20b–21*

Closing Prayer Lord God, make us strong and faithful to obey and serve you. *Amen.*

John

Light the first two purple candles and the pink candle.

Opening Prayer Lord Jesus, we rejoice in you. As we hear the familiar stories of those who lived in the days of your first coming, open our hearts to experience the joy you brought to your people when you came into the world to live among us. Fill us with hope, grant us your peace, and make us joyful. *Amen.*

Lesson The birth of John brought great joy. His parents had waited so long for a child, and the people who knew Zechariah and Elizabeth rejoiced with them when their son was born. According to Jewish custom, all the family and friends gathered together eight days after the baby boy was born to celebrate and welcome him into the family of God, and to circumcise him and give him a name.

Read Luke 1:57–80.

Zechariah had not been able to speak since the angel appeared to him in the temple. He had doubted the promise God made to him through the words of the angel, and he had asked for a sign (as though having an angel appear and speak to him wasn't enough of a sign!). The sign he was given was the loss of his voice during the months of waiting for his child to be born, and so when it was time to name his son, he had to write the name on a tablet. His friends and relatives could not believe he was not planning to give his son a family name, as was the custom. But Zechariah's obedience to God brought about his healing. The first words from his mouth came after he named his son John, as the angel had instructed. He prophesied about the coming Messiah and about his child becoming a prophet who would prepare the way for the Messiah, and he praised God for sending His people a Savior. The words Zechariah spoke are recited and sung in many church services as a song of praise called the *Benedictus*, which is Latin for "blessed."

John grew up to be a great prophet who was filled with the Holy Spirit, and he fulfilled his mission as the forerunner who prepared the way for Jesus. John was such a powerful and amazing man of God that many mistook him for the Christ. But he was quick to correct this mistake, and he spent his life leading people to Jesus.

Key Verses   "Blessed be the Lord God of Israel, for he has looked favorably on his people and redeemed them. And you, child, will be called the prophet of the Most High; for you will go before the Lord to prepare his ways." *Luke 1:68, 76 (NRSV)*

Closing Prayer   Come Holy Spirit, and prepare the way for Jesus in the hearts of your people. *Amen.*

Review

Light the first two purple candles and the pink candle.

Opening Prayer Lord Jesus, we rejoice in you. As we hear the familiar stories of those who lived in the days of your first coming, open our hearts to experience the joy you brought to your people when you came into the world to live among us. Fill us with hope, grant us your peace, and make us joyful. *Amen.*

Lesson This week we have heard stories of the people who lived during the time in which Jesus was born. It is hard for us to imagine how they all must have felt to be chosen by God to participate in such an awesome event. But one thing is clear from their stories: they felt great joy at being chosen to witness the fulfillment of God's promise to send them a Savior. When Jesus comes into our lives, He brings joy.

Read aloud the key verses for this week and experience the joy of the coming of Jesus.

Key Verses But the angel said to him: "Do not be afraid, Zechariah; your prayer has been heard. Your wife Elizabeth will bear you a son, and you are to give him the name John. He will be a joy and delight to you, and many will rejoice because of his birth." *Luke 1:13–14*

The angel answered, "The Holy Spirit will come upon you, and the power of the Most High will overshadow you. So the holy one to be born will be called the Son of God."

"I am the Lord's servant," Mary answered. "May it be to me as you have said." *Luke 1:35, 38*

And Mary said, "My soul magnifies the Lord, and my spirit rejoices in God my Savior, for he has looked with favor on the lowliness of his servant. Surely, from now on all generations will call me blessed; for the Mighty One has done great things for me, and holy is his name." *Luke 1:46–49 (NRSV)*

"Joseph son of David, do not be afraid to take Mary home as your wife, because what is conceived in her is from the Holy Spirit. She will give birth to a son, and you are to give him the name Jesus, because he will save his people from their sins." *Matthew 1:20b–21*

"Blessed be the Lord God of Israel, for he has looked favorably on his people and redeemed them. And you, child, will be called the prophet of the Most High; for you will go before the Lord to prepare his ways." *Luke 1:68, 76 (NRSV)*

Closing Prayer   Lord Jesus, our joy is complete in you. *Amen.*

Love

Read Isaiah 9:2–7 aloud, and light all three purple candles and the pink candle.

Opening Prayer   Dear God, you showed your love to us by sending your one and only Son into the world that we might live through Him. As we celebrate the birth of Jesus, fill us with hope, grant us your peace, make us joyful, and show forth your love in us. *Amen.*

Lesson   The last purple candle is called the Love candle. All of our candles are lit now except one, and our wait is almost over. In just a few days, we will light the white Christ candle in the center of our wreaths and celebrate the birth of Jesus, and we will read the story of God's amazing expression of love for His people. You will never receive a gift so great and as full of love as the gift God offers us through Jesus.

Read 1 John 4:7–12.

Closing Prayer   Father God, this is love: not that we loved you, but that you loved us, and sent your Son to save us. *Amen.*

Note: The fourth week in Advent can last from one to seven days, depending on the day of the week on which Christmas Day falls. You may choose from any of the lessons included in this week's devotions to use during the days leading up to Christmas. Just be sure to skip to the Christmas Eve lesson on December 24.

Shepherds

Light all three purple candles and the pink candle.

Opening Prayer   Dear God, you showed your love to us by sending your one and only Son into the world that we might live through Him. As we celebrate the birth of Jesus, fill us with hope, grant us your peace, make us joyful, and show forth your love in us. *Amen.*

Lesson   "And there were in the same country shepherds abiding in the field, keeping watch over their flock by night" (*Luke 2:8, KJV*). Shepherds? Did you ever wonder why God chose to make the first birth announcement of Jesus to some unknown shepherds out in the fields that night? The Bible mentions shepherds more than 200 times. Shepherding was the main occupation of the Israelites during the time of Abraham, Moses, and the other patriarchs. In the Old Testament, the word "shepherd" came to mean more than just those who cared for sheep. It was used to describe the role of kings, leaders, and even God Himself (*2 Samuel 5:2, Jeremiah 23*, and *Isaiah 40:11*). In the New Testament, our relationship with Jesus is compared to a sheep's relationship with its shepherd (*Hebrews 13:20*). And Jesus called Himself "the good shepherd" who knew His sheep and would lay down His life for them (*John 10:11–18*). When Jesus appointed Peter as a leader of the church, He said to him, "Feed my sheep" (*John 21:17*), and He meant for Peter to protect and care for His followers. Our

English word "pastor" comes from the Latin word for shepherd. King David was a shepherd, and he understood that God also thought of Himself as a shepherd.

Read Psalm 23.

It is not a compliment to be compared to a sheep, because they are not known for being the most intelligent animals. Sheep are very dependent on their shepherd. They will quickly stray into danger and be attacked by predators or wander away from the flock and starve if the shepherd does not watch them constantly and lead them to good pastures. Jesus is our Shepherd who cares for us, keeps us safe, carries us when we are weak, brings us back when we are lost, and leads us through this life and into eternal life with Him. If Jesus thinks of Himself as our shepherd, we should be happy to think of ourselves as His sheep.

Key Verses   Surely goodness and love will follow me all the days of my life, and I will dwell in the house of the Lord forever. *Psalm 23:6*

Closing Prayer   Lord Jesus, you are our Shepherd. We shall not be in want. *Amen.*

Angels

Light all three purple candles and the pink candle.

Opening Prayer Dear God, you showed your love to us by sending your one and only Son into the world that we might live through Him. As we celebrate the birth of Jesus, fill us with hope, grant us your peace, make us joyful, and show forth your love in us. *Amen.*

Lesson What was the very first thing the angel said to Zechariah, and to Mary, and to the shepherds? Fear not. Do not be afraid. There must be something fearsome about the way angels look, because they seem to have to reassure people before they can communicate their message. Angels were created by God to worship and serve Him, to carry out His will, and to act as messengers. In fact, the Hebrew and Greek words for angel both mean "messenger."

Sometimes people become so interested in angels that they forget that angels were created by God and do not act on behalf of anyone but Him. The writer of the book of Hebrews explained the position of angels in God's creation to some Jewish believers who were confused about angels.

Read Hebrews 1:1–14.

Angels are closely connected and involved with the coming of Jesus—both His first and second comings. An angel announced that He was about to be born (*Luke 1:26–33*); angels appeared to the shepherds on the night he was born (*Luke 2:9*); angels ministered to Him after his ordeal in the desert with Satan (*Matthew 4:11*); and an angel rolled back the stone from His tomb and, after terrifying the guards, explained to the women who were looking for the body of Jesus that He had risen (*Matthew 28:1–7*). Forty days later, when Jesus ascended into Heaven, two angels proclaimed that He would return one day in the same way He left. The Bible tells us that the voice of an archangel will be heard at the second coming of Jesus (*1 Thessalonians 4:16*), and Jesus said that angels will accompany Him when He returns (*Matthew 25:31*).

Key Verses   "In the beginning, O Lord, you laid the foundations of the earth, and the heavens are the work of your hands. They will perish, but you remain; they will all wear out like a garment. You will roll them up like a robe; like a garment they will be changed. But you remain the same, and your years will never end." *Hebrews 1:10–12*

Closing Prayer   Let all God's angels worship Him. *Amen.*

The Star in the East

Light all three purple candles and the pink candle.

Opening Prayer   Dear God, you showed your love to us by sending your one and only Son into the world that we might live through Him. As we celebrate the birth of Jesus, fill us with hope, grant us your peace, make us joyful, and show forth your love in us. *Amen.*

Lesson   What was the star that appeared in the sky when Jesus was born? Was it a comet? A nova? Either of these phenomena might explain the sudden appearance of the star, the sustained path it traveled, and the endurance of the star over time. God certainly is able to command the heavenly bodies to behave in a way that would attract attention. Or He could have created a new star to announce the birth of His Son. But the Gospel writer Matthew gives us a clue that the star was not a comet, a nova, or any other spectacular phenomenon that everyone would have noticed around the time of Jesus' birth. When the Magi came looking for the newborn king at Herod's palace in Jerusalem and informed him that they had followed a star to Judea, Herod had to ask them exactly when the star had appeared (*Matthew 2:7*). Surely, the appearance of a comet or a new star would have attracted the attention of many people, and yet Herod apparently had neither seen nor heard of any unusual appearance in the sky. The star might have been something that looked normal to most people until the Magi explained why it was so extraordinary.

Some modern astronomers propose that the appearance of the star was actually the alignment of the planet Jupiter with one or more existing stars. This hypothesis would explain why most people did not notice anything unusual in the night sky. The Magi, however, had been studying the ancient prophecies about the coming of a king to the Jewish people, and they recognized the star as a sign that the prophecies were coming to pass. The star proved to be a reliable guide for their journey to Bethlehem, leading them directly to Jesus and His parents. Whatever the origin of the star, God used it to draw those He had chosen to be among the early witnesses of the first coming of Christ. Furthermore, Jesus said that signs in the sun, moon, and stars will indicate that His second coming is near (*Luke 21:25*).

Read Psalm 19.

Key Verses The heavens declare the glory of God; the skies proclaim the work of his hands. *Psalm 19:1*

Closing Prayer O God, you set the stars in the sky, and the heavens declare your glory. *Amen.*

The Manger

Light all three purple candles and the pink candle.

Opening Prayer   Dear God, you showed your love to us by sending your one and only Son into the world that we might live through Him. As we celebrate the birth of Jesus, fill us with hope, grant us your peace, make us joyful, and show forth your love in us. *Amen.*

Lesson   The story and the setting of Jesus' birth is one of the ways God demonstrates to us that the Kingdom of Heaven is unlike any earthly kingdom we know. We might expect that the Word made flesh, the Creator of the universe, would have been born into opulent surroundings with royal dignitaries to welcome Him. But Jesus was born in a stable and laid in a manger, with only His parents and the animals to witness His birth.

Many times the lack of a cradle has prompted desperate parents to place their babies in unusual places such as dresser drawers or bathtubs. But a manger is a feeding trough for animals and surely was not very clean. And these were no ordinary parents. Mary and Joseph were chosen by God to care for the promised Messiah. But when the time came for the baby to be born, the couple found themselves in a humble stable with only a manger in which to place their newborn.

When Jesus was much older, he went to a dinner party given by a very important man. He told the guests a story to teach them about humility.

Read Luke 14:7–11.

When Jesus arrived as a baby, he certainly did take the lowest place. He could have been born in the palace in Jerusalem just a few miles away. There he could have grown up with power and wealth so that he could use his influence to make people listen to his message. But he seems to have chosen the lowest place he could think of. The King of kings and the Lord of lords was born in a stable and placed in a manger.

Key Verses For everyone who exalts himself will be humbled, and he who humbles himself will be exalted. *Luke 14:11*

Closing Prayer Lord Jesus, we humble ourselves before you. You are highly exalted forever and ever. *Amen.*

Review

Light all three purple candles and the pink candle.

Opening Prayer
Dear God, you showed your love to us by sending your one and only Son into the world that we might live through Him. As we celebrate the birth of Jesus, fill us with hope, grant us your peace, make us joyful, and show forth your love in us. *Amen.*

Lesson
The shepherds, the angels, the star, and even the manger, all set the stage for the first coming of the Messiah. Review the key verses from this week's lessons, and prepare to read the story of Jesus' birth on Christmas Eve.

Key Verses
Surely goodness and love will follow me all the days of my life, and I will dwell in the house of the Lord forever. *Psalm 23:6*

"In the beginning, O Lord, you laid the foundations of the earth, and the heavens are the work of your hands. They will perish, but you remain; they will all wear out like a garment. You will roll them up like a robe; like a garment they will be changed. But you remain the same, and your years will never end." *Hebrews 1:10–12*

The heavens declare the glory of God; the skies proclaim the work of his hands. *Psalm 19:1*

For everyone who exalts himself will be humbled, and he who humbles himself will be exalted. *Luke 14:11*

Closing Prayer   Father God, this is love: not that we loved you, but that you loved us, and sent your Son to save us. *Amen.*

The Birth of Jesus

Light all the candles in your wreath, including the white Christ candle in the center.

Opening Prayer Dear God, you showed your love to us by sending your one and only Son into the world that we might live through Him. As we celebrate the birth of Jesus, fill us with hope, grant us your peace, make us joyful, and show forth your love in us. *Amen.*

Lesson *Read Luke 2:1–20.*

Key Verses And the angel said unto them, Fear not: for, behold, I bring you good tidings of great joy, which shall be to all people. For unto you is born this day in the city of David a Saviour, which is Christ the Lord. And this shall be a sign unto you; Ye shall find the babe wrapped in swaddling clothes, lying in a manger. And suddenly there was with the angel a multitude of the heavenly host praising God, and saying, Glory to God in the highest, and on earth peace, good will toward men. *Luke 2:10–14 (KJV)*

Closing Glory to God in the highest, and on earth peace,
Prayer good will toward men. *Amen.*

The Word Became Flesh

Read John 1:14 aloud, and light only the white Christ candle. (Advent is over; Christmas has come. You may remove the Advent candles from your wreath if you wish.)

Opening Prayer   Dear God, you showed your love to us by sending your one and only Son into the world that we might live through Him. As we celebrate the birth of Jesus, fill us with hope, grant us your peace, make us joyful, and show forth your love in us. *Amen.*

Lesson   Merry Christmas! You have been hearing those words for weeks now. And soon the stores will take down their decorations, the radio stations will stop playing Christmas music, and most people will forget about Christmas. But really, today is only the first day of Christmas. It's not over. It has only just begun.

The scene was probably the same in many homes this morning. Did you come running into the room where the presents were left? Did you tear open the wrapping paper, hoping to find that perfect gift? Were you thrilled when you received exactly what you wanted? Or have you discovered already that the things you thought would make you happy have failed to satisfy you for very long?

The gift that God gave us on the first Christmas was the perfect gift, and it will never break or disappoint us. Jesus came, and He will never leave us. Long after the tree and the decorations come down, the presents are put aside, and the holidays are forgotten, Jesus is still there with us. His presence in our lives—and the hope, peace, joy, and love that He brings—are always there for those who believe and accept Him as Savior. We should never forget the message of Christmas. Once Jesus came into the world, things were never the same again. Once He comes into our lives, we are never the same again.

Our wait is over—Christmas is here. Today we will read one of the same passages of scripture with which we began the first week in Advent. Listen again, and see how God has prepared your heart this season for the coming of Jesus.

Read John 1:1–14.

Key Verses The Word became flesh and made his dwelling among us. We have seen his glory, the glory of the One and Only, who came from the Father, full of grace and truth. *John 1:14*

Closing Prayer Lord Jesus, you came. And we will never be the same again. *Amen.*

Simeon and Anna

Light the white Christ candle.

Opening Prayer Dear God, you showed your love to us by sending your one and only Son into the world that we might live through Him. As we celebrate the birth of Jesus, fill us with hope, grant us your peace, make us joyful, and show forth your love in us. *Amen.*

Lesson Does it seem like you waited a long time for Christmas to arrive this year? Today we will read about two people who waited a very long time for the first Christmas.

Read Luke 2:21–38.

God had promised Simeon that he would not die before he had seen the promised Christ, and so Simeon had watched and waited. When Joseph and Mary brought Jesus into the temple, God revealed to Simeon that Jesus was the promised One. Simeon felt his life was now complete and nothing could ever top this experience. He told God that now he could die in peace because he had seen all he ever needed to see. His prayer is called "The Song of Simeon" or the *Nunc Dimittis*, which is Latin for "now you dismiss." Simeon was overjoyed to see Jesus, but when he spoke to Mary about her child, we hear the first note of sadness connected to the coming of Jesus and a foreshadowing of the suffering He would endure.

Anna was also in the temple that day. In fact, Luke tells us she never left the temple but stayed there day and night, fasting and praying. She had watched and waited almost her entire life to see the promised Messiah, and here He was. She was so happy to see Jesus, she praised God and told everyone around her that the Savior had come.

Key Verses   "Sovereign Lord, as you have promised, you now dismiss your servant in peace. For my eyes have seen your salvation, which you have prepared in the sight of all people, a light for revelation to the Gentiles and for glory to your people Israel." *Luke 2:29–32*

Closing Prayer   Sovereign Lord, we have seen your salvation. *Amen.*

Jesus in the Temple

Light the white Christ candle.

Opening Prayer Dear God, you showed your love to us by sending your one and only Son into the world that we might live through Him. As we celebrate the birth of Jesus, fill us with hope, grant us your peace, make us joyful, and show forth your love in us. *Amen.*

Lesson We know that eventually Joseph and Mary returned with Jesus to Nazareth. The Bible does not tell us very much about His childhood, but we can assume that He grew up much like any other Jewish boy. The only glimpse we have into the early years of Jesus' life is an event that took place when He was 12.

Read Luke 2:39–52.

We read yesterday that Mary and Joseph brought Jesus to the temple eight days after His birth to be circumcised and named according to the Jewish custom. They returned to the temple 40 days after Jesus was born to offer a sacrifice for purification— also a Jewish law. This was the occasion on which they met Simeon and Anna.

Joseph and Mary did everything required of them by the Law that God had given Moses for the Jewish people. Even though they had been entrusted with the awesome responsibility of raising Jesus, they did not see themselves as deserving special privileges or as being exempt from the Law. They celebrated the Feast of the Passover every year as was the custom, and on this particular year, they unknowingly left Jesus in Jerusalem. Mary and Joseph made mistakes like all parents, but Jesus was perfectly obedient to them. From this passage we can see that Jesus was aware that He was God's Son at a young age, and yet He fulfilled all the expectations of His human position in life as the eldest son in a Jewish family. He learned the trade of his earthly father, and when he was grown, he made His living as a carpenter. We hear nothing more about Jesus until he began His public ministry around the age of 30.

Key Verses
And the child grew and became strong; he was filled with wisdom, and the grace of God was upon him. *Luke 2:40*

Closing Prayer
Lord Jesus, help us to be obedient as you were obedient. *Amen.*

Review

Light the white Christ candle.

Opening Prayer
Dear God, you showed your love to us by sending your one and only Son into the world that we might live through Him. As we celebrate the birth of Jesus, fill us with hope, grant us your peace, make us joyful, and show forth your love in us. *Amen.*

Lesson
Try not to allow the world to convince you that Christmas is over. Read once again some of our key verses, and continue to celebrate the amazing love of God in the gift of Jesus.

Key Verses
And the angel said unto them, Fear not: for, behold, I bring you good tidings of great joy, which shall be to all people. For unto you is born this day in the city of David a Saviour, which is Christ the Lord. And this shall be a sign unto you; Ye shall find the babe wrapped in swaddling clothes, lying in a manger. And suddenly there was with the angel a multitude of the heavenly host praising God, and saying, Glory to God in the highest, and on earth peace, good will toward men. *Luke 2:10–14 (KJV)*

The Word became flesh and made his dwelling among us. We have seen his glory, the glory of the One and Only, who came from the Father, full of grace and truth. *John 1:14*

"Sovereign Lord, as you have promised, you now dismiss your servant in peace. For my eyes have seen your salvation, which you have prepared in the sight of all people, a light for revelation to the Gentiles and for glory to your people Israel." *Luke 2:29–32*

And the child grew and became strong; he was filled with wisdom, and the grace of God was upon Him. *Luke 2:40*

Closing Glory to God in the highest, and on earth peace,
Prayer good will toward men. *Amen.*

Jesus Is Coming Again

Light the white Christ candle.

Opening Prayer Lord Jesus, we celebrate your birth, and we look forward to your coming again. Your whole creation waits for you with eager expectation. Strengthen our hearts so that we will be holy and blameless in the presence of God the Father when you come. Teach us how to live. *Amen.*

Lesson We have been celebrating the birth of Jesus—His first coming. But from the very beginning, from the earliest prophecies of the coming of the Christ, we have known that Jesus is coming again. When Jesus came the first time, He made it clear to His disciples that He would come back one day.

Read Matthew 24:26–44.

It is hard to imagine what the second coming of Jesus will be like, but one thing is certain: the second coming will not be like the first. Jesus will not be born as a child into a family who is expecting Him. He will come with the angels in all His glory, and He will come suddenly, at a time when we are not expecting Him.

Key Verses Therefore keep watch, because you do not know on what day your Lord will come. *Matthew 24:42*

Closing Lord Jesus, only the Father knows the day of your
Prayer coming. Help us to keep watch. *Amen.*

God Is Not Slow

Light the white Christ candle.

Opening Prayer Lord Jesus, we celebrate your birth, and we look forward to your coming again. Your whole creation waits for you with eager expectation. Strengthen our hearts so that we will be holy and blameless in the presence of God the Father when you come. Teach us how to live. *Amen.*

Lesson How long has it been since Jesus was born? Over 2000 years! That seems like a long time, doesn't it? The Jewish people also waited for centuries for Jesus to come. Some of them probably gave up and forgot about the prophecies that foretold the coming of the Messiah. And now we are waiting for Him to come again. He came the first time just as God promised, and He will come again. We cannot forget or give up, no matter how long we have to wait.

Read 2 Peter 3:1–14.

God is not slow. It may seem like He is taking a long time to come, but this is only because He wants all of us to come to Him. We are His creation, and we do not experience time in the same way He does. We have read that God said His name is "I AM." He is the God who was, who is, and who is to come. Jesus was with God when we were created. He has always been, and He will always be. He will keep His promise, and Jesus will come again.

Key Verses But do not forget this one thing, dear friends: With the Lord a day is like a thousand years, and a thousand years are like a day. The Lord is not slow in keeping his promise, as some understand slowness. He is patient with you, not wanting anyone to perish, but everyone to come to repentance. *2 Peter 3:8–9*

Closing Prayer Lord, you are not slow in keeping your promise. You will come. *Amen.*

Waiting

Light the white Christ candle.

Opening Prayer Lord Jesus, we celebrate your birth, and we look forward to your coming again. Your whole creation waits for you with eager expectation. Strengthen our hearts so that we will be holy and blameless in the presence of God the Father when you come. Teach us how to live. *Amen.*

Lesson What should we do while we are waiting for Jesus to come again?

Read Titus 2:11–14.

Jesus has come, and He is our salvation. By God's grace we have been saved. We did not do anything to earn our salvation, but rather God gives it to us freely through Jesus. To those who believe in Jesus, He has given the Holy Spirit to show us how to live by faith while we wait for Jesus to come again. We cannot live self-controlled, upright, and godly lives in our own strength. We do not have the wisdom, the power, or the goodness within us naturally to live a life pleasing to God. We must rely on Him to show us how to live, and trust in the power of the Holy Spirit to accomplish the good things God calls us to do in our lives.

Key Verses   For the grace of God that brings salvation has appeared to all men. It teaches us to say "No" to ungodliness and worldly passions, and to live self-controlled, upright and godly lives in this present age, while we wait for the blessed hope—the glorious appearing of our great God and Savior, Jesus Christ. *Titus 2:11–13*

Closing Prayer   Lord God, we rely on your grace as we wait for the glorious appearing of Jesus. *Amen.*

Growing

Light the white Christ candle.

Opening Prayer Lord Jesus, we celebrate your birth, and we look forward to your coming again. Your whole creation waits for you with eager expectation. Strengthen our hearts so that we will be holy and blameless in the presence of God the Father when you come. Teach us how to live. *Amen.*

Lesson What else should we do while we wait?

Read Philippians 1:3–11.

God's power is working in us while we wait for Jesus for come. We are not only to be patient and self-controlled, but we also are to keep growing, maturing, and learning about what it means to be a follower of Jesus. When we believe that Jesus is the Son of God, the Holy Spirit begins to work in us, giving us the wisdom to know what is right and the power to live a life pleasing to God. It is not from our own strength and effort that we become more holy; it is the power of God through the Holy Spirit working in us to make us more like Jesus. This is what we do while we wait: we allow God to make us more and more like Jesus.

Key Verses He who began a good work in you will carry it on to completion until the day of Christ Jesus. *Philippians 1:6b*

**Closing
Prayer**   Lord Jesus, complete your work in us. *Amen.*

Come, Lord Jesus

Light the white Christ candle.

Opening Prayer Lord Jesus, we celebrate your birth, and we look forward to your coming again. Your whole creation waits for you with eager expectation. Strengthen our hearts so that we will be holy and blameless in the presence of God the Father when you come. Teach us how to live. *Amen.*

Lesson During Advent we read about God's promise to send a Savior, how He spoke through the prophets about the coming of Jesus, and how the people waited for Him to come. Advent means "coming." At Christmas we celebrate the fulfillment of God's promise in the birth of Jesus. Jesus did come, and now we are waiting for Him to come again.

Read Revelation 22:12–21.

All through the ages, God's people have entreated Him to come to them. But He also has called us to come to *Him*. Jesus said, "Come to me, all you who are weary and burdened, and I will give you rest" (*Matthew 11:28*) and "I am the way and the truth and the life. No one comes to the Father except through me" (*John 14:6*). In fact, it was Jesus who called first. We love Him because He first loved us. We desire Him to come because He first called us to come.

In the beginning, Jesus was with God. Jesus IS God. He is the Great I AM; the one who was, and is, and is to come; the Alpha and the Omega, the First and the Last, the Beginning and the End. And He calls us to come to Him.

Key Verses   "Behold, I am coming soon! My reward is with me, and I will give to everyone according to what he has done. I am the Alpha and the Omega, the First and the Last, the Beginning and the End." Whoever is thirsty, let him come; and whoever wishes, let him take the free gift of the water of life. *Revelation 22:12–13, 17b*

Closing Prayer   Amen. Come, Lord Jesus. The grace of the Lord Jesus be with God's people. *Amen.*

Review

Light the white Christ candle.

Opening Prayer Lord Jesus, we celebrate your birth, and we look forward to your coming again. Your whole creation waits for you with eager expectation. Strengthen our hearts so that we will be holy and blameless in the presence of God the Father when you come. Teach us how to live. *Amen.*

Lesson We are nearing the end of Christmas, and you might be wondering what happened to the wise men. We have not forgotten about them. We usually read about the wise men, called the Magi, at the beginning of Epiphany, which is the season that begins on January 6. The word *epiphany* comes from a Greek verb that means "to show, appear, or make known." God appeared and made Himself known to all the world when Jesus was born. In our language, people use the word *epiphany* to describe a feeling of sudden realization or understanding of something very important. The symbol of the season of Epiphany is light. God led the wise men to Jesus by the light of a star, and when they arrived in Bethlehem, they discovered the Messiah and understood that He was the One they were looking for. Jesus is the light of the world, and God is calling all people to come to Him through Jesus.

Today we will review the key verses about the second coming of Jesus. Then during the last two days of Christmas, we will read more about the Magi.

Key Verses Therefore keep watch, because you do not know on what day your Lord will come. *Matthew 24:42*

But do not forget this one thing, dear friends: With the Lord a day is like a thousand years, and a thousand years are like a day. The Lord is not slow in keeping his promise, as some understand slowness. He is patient with you, not wanting anyone to perish, but everyone to come to repentance. *2 Peter 3:8–9*

For the grace of God that brings salvation has appeared to all men. It teaches us to say "No" to ungodliness and worldly passions, and to live self-controlled, upright and godly lives in this present age, while we wait for the blessed hope—the glorious appearing of our great God and Savior, Jesus Christ. *Titus 2:11–13*

He who began a good work in you will carry it on to completion until the day of Christ Jesus. *Philippians 1:6b*

"Behold, I am coming soon! My reward is with me, and I will give to everyone according to what he has done. I am the Alpha and the Omega, the First and the Last, the Beginning and the End." Whoever is thirsty, let him come; and whoever wishes, let him take the free gift of the water of life. *Revelation 22:12–13, 17b*

Closing Prayer Lord Jesus, you are coming soon. *Amen.*

The Magi

Light the white Christ candle.

Opening Prayer   Lord God, you led the wise men to Jesus by the light of a star. May the light of Jesus so shine in us that all the world may know you and the One you sent. Send us forth into the world to proclaim the message of Christmas—Christ has come, and He will come again. *Amen.*

Lesson   The Magi were an ancient order of priests who came from somewhere east of Jerusalem. They studied ancient writings, mapped out the stars, interpreted dreams, and were considered to be scholarly, which is why we call them "The Wise Men." Many people assume there were three wise men because they brought three gifts, but we really do not know how many came to see Jesus. If they came from Persia or Babylon, they probably had access to a copy of the Jewish Law and the writings of the Old Testament prophets, because the Jewish people had lived there as captives several hundred years earlier. The Magi had been studying the ancient prophecies about the coming of a King and watching the stars for a sign that the prophecies were coming to pass. God used the appearance of a star in the eastern sky to convince them that the fulfillment of the prophecies was near and to lead them to Jesus.

Read Matthew 2:1–11.

We might not know exactly who they were, or where they came from, or even how many of them there were, but we do know that the Magi were not Jewish. The Jewish leaders in Jerusalem knew well the prophecies of the coming Messiah, even that He was to be born in Bethlehem. And yet, the Magi journeyed on alone from Jerusalem, and the Jews did not accompany them to seek Jesus.

From the very beginning, God has been calling people of all nations to come to Him through Jesus. The prophet Isaiah, when he spoke of the future redeemer of Israel, said, "I will also make you a light for the Gentiles, that you may bring my salvation to the ends of the earth" (*Isaiah 49:6b*). And when Simeon saw Jesus in the temple, he said, "For my eyes have seen your salvation, which you have prepared in the sight of all people, a light for revelation to the Gentiles and for glory to your people Israel" (*Luke 2:30–32*). Paul, a first century Jewish leader who was called by God to take the gospel message to the Gentiles, said that "the Gentiles are heirs together with Israel, members together of one body, and sharers together in the promise in Christ Jesus" (*Ephesians 3:6*).

Key Verses   "Where is the one who has been born king of the Jews? We saw his star in the east and have come to worship him." *Matthew 2:2*

Closing Prayer   Lord Jesus, wise men of all nations seek you and hail you as King. *Amen.*

Home by Another Way

Light the white Christ candle.

Opening Prayer Lord God, you led the wise men to Jesus by the light of a star. May the light of Jesus so shine in us that all the world may know you and the One you sent. Send us forth into the world to proclaim the message of Christmas—Christ has come, and He will come again. *Amen.*

Lesson The ancient Romans are famous for the roads they built. The geographical region in which Jesus was born is a major crossroads of three continents, and under the rule of the Roman Empire, the roads leading in and out of Jerusalem and Bethlehem were well guarded and safe to travel. The wise men probably traveled a long way to find Jesus, but the journey would not have been particularly hard by that day's standard. God prepared the way for the wise men to find Jesus, not only by leaving the prophecies of the coming Messiah in their own land for them to discover, but also by leading them right to the place where Jesus was born.

God also prepared the way for Joseph and Mary. We know that they did not have much money, because the offering they made for Mary's purification was a small one that only very poor people were allowed to make. God provided for Joseph and Mary by sending the wise men with gifts that were very valuable. This provision would have sustained them while they fled to Egypt to escape Herod's awful plot to kill Jesus.

Read Matthew 2:12–23.

Joseph and Mary's journey to Bethlehem did not turn out as they had planned. They were gone much longer than they expected, and they had to return home by a different way. After the wise men discovered Jesus, God warned them not to go back to Herod, and they also had to find a different route back to their home country.

Life's journey rarely turns out as we had planned. But God has prepared the way for us to return to Him, and that way is Jesus. When we discover who Jesus really is and what He offers us, we also are brought to a major crossroads. We can continue on as we had planned, or we can change our direction and follow Jesus. Perhaps you have discovered for the first time this year the real meaning of Christmas. We have come to the end of this part of our journey. Will you, like the wise men, return home by another way?

Key Verses   And being warned of God in a dream that they should not return to Herod, they departed into their own country another way. *Matthew 2:12 (KJV)*

Closing Prayer   Lord Jesus, we have seen your glory, the glory of the One and Only, who came from the Father, full of grace and truth. Lead us home by another way. *Amen.*

Key Verses

In the beginning was the Word, and the Word was with God, and the Word was God. He was with God in the beginning. Through him all things were made; without him nothing was made that has been made. *John 1:1–3*

So God created man in his own image, in the image of God he created him; male and female he created them. *Genesis 1:27*

The Lord had said to Abram,
"I will make you into a great nation and I will bless you; I will make your name great, and you will be a blessing. I will bless those who bless you, and whoever curses you I will curse; and all peoples on earth will be blessed through you." *Genesis 12:1a, 2–3*

God said to Moses, "I AM WHO I AM. This is my name forever, the name by which I am to be remembered from generation to generation." *Exodus 3:14a, 15b*

Then King David went in and sat before the Lord, and he said: "And now, Lord God, keep forever the promise you have made concerning your servant and his house. Do as you promised, so that your name will be great forever. Then men will say, 'The Lord Almighty is God over Israel!' And the house of your servant David will be established before you." *2 Samuel 7:18a, 25–26*

"Come, let us go up to the mountain of the Lord, to the house of the God of Jacob. He will teach us his ways, so that we may walk in his paths." *Isaiah 2:3*

A shoot will come up from the stump of Jesse; from his roots a Branch will bear fruit. *Isaiah 11:1*

Therefore the Lord himself will give you a sign: The virgin will be with child and will give birth to a son, and will call him Immanuel. *Isaiah 7:14*

"But you, Bethlehem Ephrathah, though you are small among the clans of Judah, out of you will come for me one who will be ruler over Israel, whose origins are from of old, from ancient times." *Micah 5:2*

A voice of one calling: "In the desert prepare the way for the Lord; make straight in the wilderness a highway for our God. Every valley shall be raised up, every mountain and hill made low; the rough ground shall become level, the rugged places a plain. And the glory of the Lord will be revealed, and all mankind together will see it. For the mouth the Lord has spoken." *Isaiah 40:3–5*

But the angel said to him: "Do not be afraid, Zechariah; your prayer has been heard. Your wife Elizabeth will bear you a son, and you are to give him the name John. He will be a joy and delight to you, and many will rejoice because of his birth." *Luke 1:13–14*

The angel answered, "The Holy Spirit will come upon you, and the power of the Most High will overshadow you. So the holy one to be born will be called the Son of God."
"I am the Lord's servant," Mary answered. "May it be to me as you have said." *Luke 1:35, 38*

And Mary said, "My soul magnifies the Lord, and my spirit rejoices in God my Savior, for he has looked with favor on the lowliness of his servant. Surely, from now on all generations will call me blessed; for the Mighty One has done great things for me, and holy is his name." *Luke 1:46–49 (NRSV)*

"Joseph son of David, do not be afraid to take Mary home as your wife, because what is conceived in her is from the Holy Spirit. She will give birth to a son, and you are to give him the name Jesus, because he will save his people from their sins." *Matthew 1:20b–21*

"Blessed be the Lord God of Israel, for he has looked favorably on his people and redeemed them. And you, child, will be called the prophet of the Most High; for you will go before the Lord to prepare his ways." *Luke 1:68, 76 (NRSV)*

Surely goodness and love will follow me all the days of my life, and I will dwell in the house of the Lord forever. *Psalm 23:6*

"In the beginning, O Lord, you laid the foundations of the earth, and the heavens are the work of your hands. They will perish, but you remain; they will all wear out like a garment. You will roll them up like a robe; like a garment they will be changed. But you remain the same, and your years will never end." *Hebrews 1:10–12*

The heavens declare the glory of God; the skies proclaim the work of his hands. *Psalm 19:1*

For everyone who exalts himself will be humbled, and he who humbles himself will be exalted. *Luke 14:11*

And the angel said unto them, Fear not: for, behold, I bring you good tidings of great joy, which shall be to all people. For unto you is born this day in the city of David a Saviour, which is Christ the Lord. And this shall be a sign unto you; Ye shall find the babe wrapped in swaddling clothes, lying in a manger. And suddenly there was with the angel a multitude of the heavenly host praising God, and saying, Glory to God in the highest, and on earth peace, good will toward men. *Luke 2:10–14 (KJV)*

The Word became flesh and made his dwelling among us. We have seen his glory, the glory of the One and Only, who came from the Father, full of grace and truth. *John 1:14*

"Sovereign Lord, as you have promised, you now dismiss your servant in peace. For my eyes have seen your salvation, which you have prepared in the sight of all people, a light for revelation to the Gentiles and for glory to your people Israel." *Luke 2:29–32*

And the child grew and became strong; he was filled with wisdom, and the grace of God was upon Him. *Luke 2:40*

Therefore keep watch, because you do not know on what day your Lord will come. *Matthew 24:42*

But do not forget this one thing, dear friends: With the Lord a day is like a thousand years, and a thousand years are like a day. The Lord is not slow in keeping his promise, as some understand slowness. He is patient with you, not wanting anyone to perish, but everyone to come to repentance. *2 Peter 3:8–9*

For the grace of God that brings salvation has appeared to all men. It teaches us to say "No" to ungodliness and worldly passions, and to live self-controlled, upright and godly lives in this present age, while we wait for the blessed hope—the glorious appearing of our great God and Savior, Jesus Christ. *Titus 2:11–13*

He who began a good work in you will carry it on to completion until the day of Christ Jesus. *Philippians 1:6b*

"Behold, I am coming soon! My reward is with me, and I will give to everyone according to what he has done. I am the Alpha and the Omega, the First and the Last, the Beginning and the End." Whoever is thirsty, let him come; and whoever wishes, let him take the free gift of the water of life. *Revelation 22:12–13, 17b*

"Where is the one who has been born king of the Jews? We saw his star in the east and have come to worship him." *Matthew 2:2*

And being warned of God in a dream that they should not return to Herod, they departed into their own country another way. *Matthew 2:12 (KJV)*

Glory to God in the highest,
and on earth peace,
good will toward men.

Luke 2:14

6659561R0

Made in the USA
Charleston, SC
19 November 2010